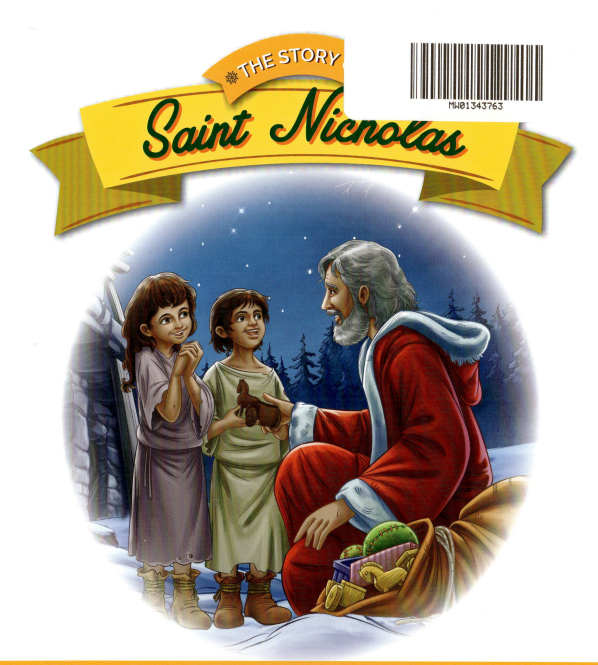

THE STORY OF Saint Nicholas

A story of humble generosity

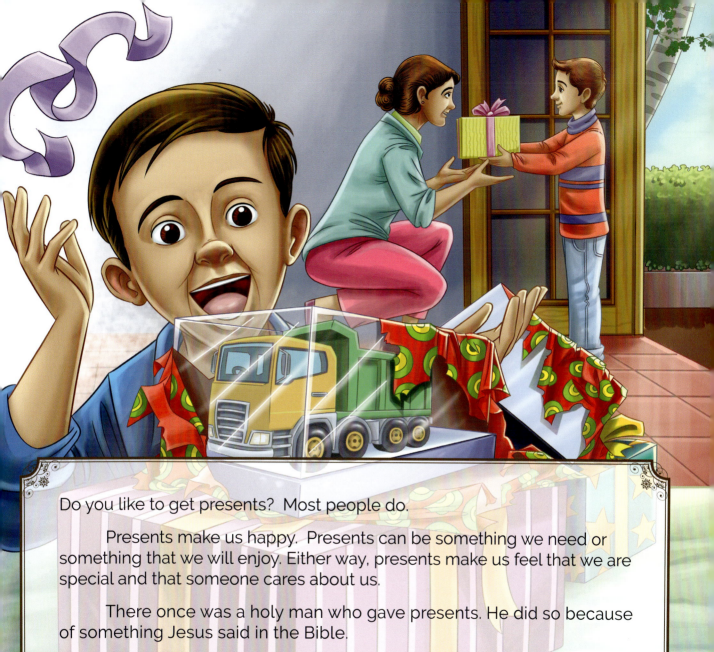

Do you like to get presents? Most people do.

Presents make us happy. Presents can be something we need or something that we will enjoy. Either way, presents make us feel that we are special and that someone cares about us.

There once was a holy man who gave presents. He did so because of something Jesus said in the Bible.

This is his story.

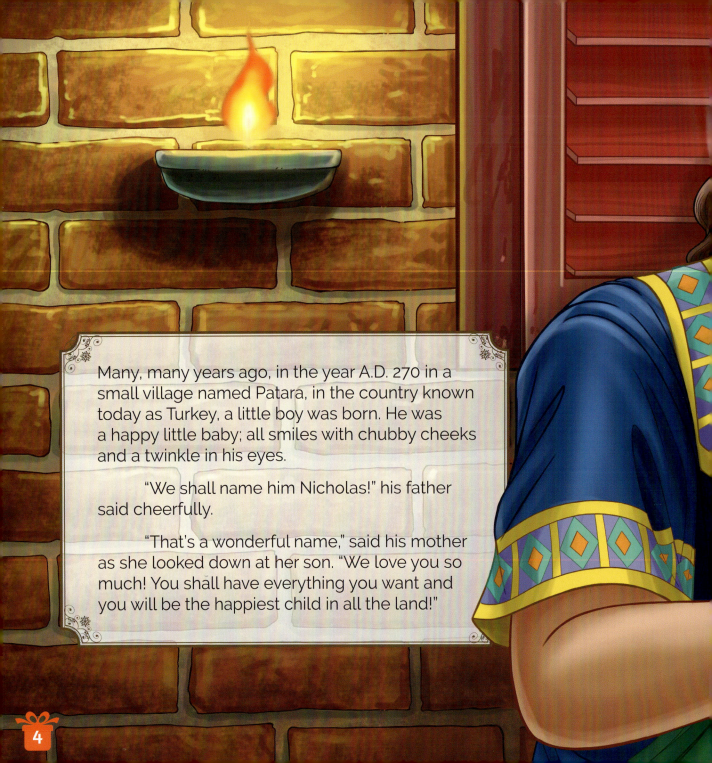

Many, many years ago, in the year A.D. 270 in a small village named Patara, in the country known today as Turkey, a little boy was born. He was a happy little baby; all smiles with chubby cheeks and a twinkle in his eyes.

"We shall name him Nicholas!" his father said cheerfully.

"That's a wonderful name," said his mother as she looked down at her son. "We love you so much! You shall have everything you want and you will be the happiest child in all the land!"

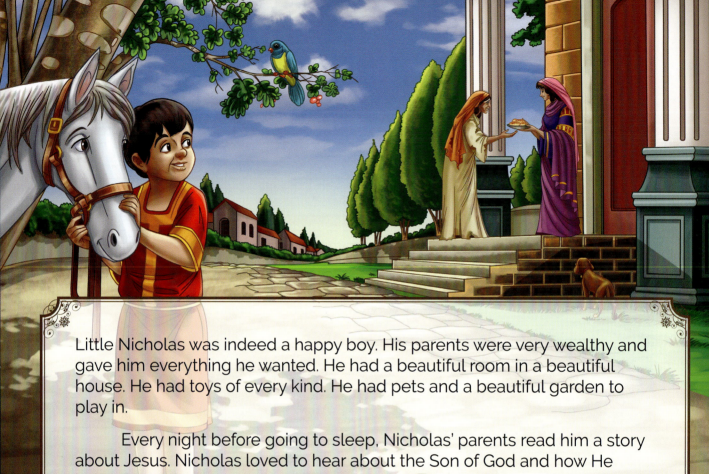

Little Nicholas was indeed a happy boy. His parents were very wealthy and gave him everything he wanted. He had a beautiful room in a beautiful house. He had toys of every kind. He had pets and a beautiful garden to play in.

Every night before going to sleep, Nicholas' parents read him a story about Jesus. Nicholas loved to hear about the Son of God and how He helped people.

"Freely you have received, so freely give!" Jesus said.

Nicholas thought about that. His parents were always helping anyone in need. He saw how happy that made them and how happy it made others.

After a prayer, his mother and father would kiss Nicholas and tuck him in.

"I am so happy!" Nicholas would say to himself as he fell asleep.

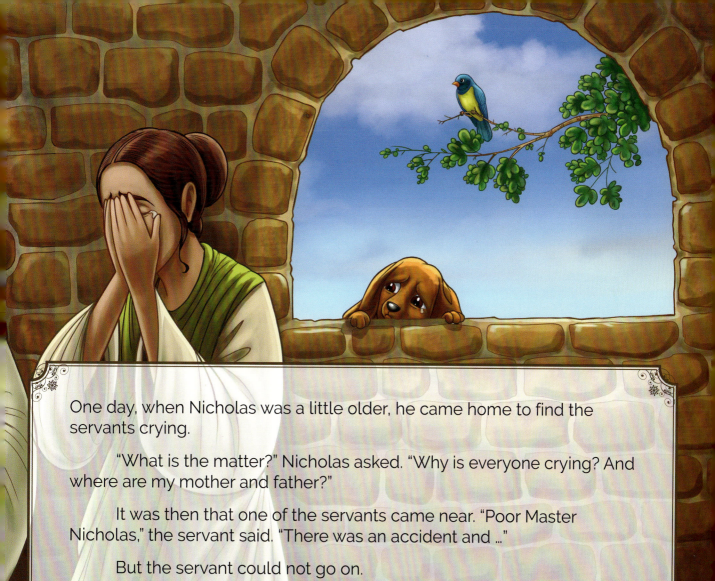

One day, when Nicholas was a little older, he came home to find the servants crying.

"What is the matter?" Nicholas asked. "Why is everyone crying? And where are my mother and father?"

It was then that one of the servants came near. "Poor Master Nicholas," the servant said. "There was an accident and …"

But the servant could not go on.

"There was an accident and what?" Nicholas asked.

"Your parents," replied the tearful servant. "They have died."

Nicholas could not believe it. How could he ever be happy again?

Days later, Nicholas sat at the table, eating by himself. His parents had left him all of their money, so Nicholas was now very rich but he was also very unhappy.

"What should I do?" he thought out loud. Just then there was a knock at the door.

"Please, can you help me with some bread?" a poor beggar lady asked as she stood outside.

Nicholas looked at the ragged clothes she wore. He looked at the two children that came with her. The little boy had no shoes and the little girl looked very cold and sad.

Then Nicholas remembered how his parents would help people in need. He remembered what Jesus said: "Freely you have received, so freely give!"

Nicholas turned to the poor people. "Would you like to have dinner with me?" he asked.

What a feast it was! The poor woman and her children ate like never before. Not only that, but Nicholas gave the children shoes and cloaks. He also gave the woman one of his mother's capes. The beggars could hardly believe it. Then Nicholas did something even more special—he gave the children some of his toys.

"Oh!" said the poor boy. "The shoes will help our feet and the cloak will keep us warm, but... why are you giving us your toys?"

Nicholas smiled. "The toys are to make you happy!" he said.

That night, as Nicholas was saying his prayers, he realized he had something to be thankful for. Although he had given away some of his clothes and toys, he felt very happy inside. He remembered something else that Jesus said: "It is more blessed to give than to receive."

Nicholas smiled. He had an idea.

"Master Nicholas!" one of the servants exclaimed as they saw the boy carrying out a wagon of clothes, toys and food. "What are you doing?"

"I am doing as God has shown me," Nicholas said. "I am going to share my blessings with the poor!"

Day after day Nicholas did the same thing. He had a lot to give away, and God blessed him with great joy as he shared with others.

One day, Nicholas heard about a man that had three daughters who were ready for marriage, but the poor man had a problem.

"What can I do? I have no money for my daughters' weddings! Dear Lord, please help me!" the man prayed.

That night, Nicholas took a bag of gold and tossed it through the man's window. Then he left before anyone could see him.

The next morning, the poor man got up and nearly stumbled over the little bag on the floor. "What is this?" he questioned as he opened it. He peeked inside, and rubbed his eyes. He looked inside again, and then he let out a very loud yell!

"God has answered my prayers!" he shouted. "God has answered my prayers!"

Soon the man's daughters came into the room to see what was happening. When they saw the bag of gold, they too began to thank God.

"What a blessing it is to give," Nicholas said to himself as he watched from a distance. "My heart is full of joy!"

Years passed, and soon Nicholas had given away everything he owned. He left his hometown and made his way to the Holy Land. Kneeling in front of Jesus' empty tomb, he bowed his head and prayed: "Dear Jesus, I have given away all I have, and You have filled me with great joy! There is one more thing I have to give. I give myself to You."

Now Nicholas belonged to God. "Do whatever You want to do with me," he prayed

On his way back from the Holy Land, Nicholas boarded a ship. But soon after they set sail, they met with a big storm! The rain pounded, the waves rose higher, and the people on the ship were very scared. "We're going to sink!" they cried out.

"Please help us, Lord!" Nicholas prayed.

Not long after, the storm passed, the waters became calm, and the ship came into port at a place called Myra.

Thankful for the Lord's answer to prayer, Nicholas ran to the nearest church to give God thanks for saving him and everyone on the ship.

What Nicholas didn't know was that some of the people of the city had gathered there to decide who should be their next bishop. They had prayed, "Dear Lord, please choose a bishop for us." They believed that the next man to come into the church would be God's chosen man.

Just then, Nicholas burst in.

"The Lord has answered our prayers!" the people shouted out.

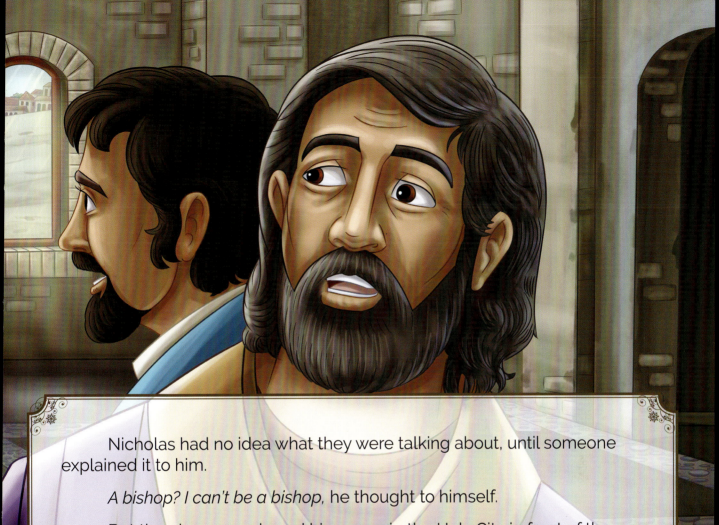

Nicholas had no idea what they were talking about, until someone explained it to him.

A bishop? I can't be a bishop, he thought to himself.

But then he remembered his prayer in the Holy City in front of the empty tomb of Christ. There he had given himself to God.

Maybe God is asking this of me. Maybe He wants me to help these people, Nicholas thought.

Nicholas took time to pray, and not long after, he was made Bishop of Myra.

For years, the good bishop did his best to be a help to the church in Myra, and the people loved him. Nicholas was a good example of Christ. He gave of his time freely and never refused anyone that needed help. He never had much, but what he did have, he shared.

Things were going well and the church was growing, when one day, the Roman emperor made a very big announcement.

"No one is allowed to teach about Christ anymore!" he commanded. "Gather all the Christian books and burn them!"

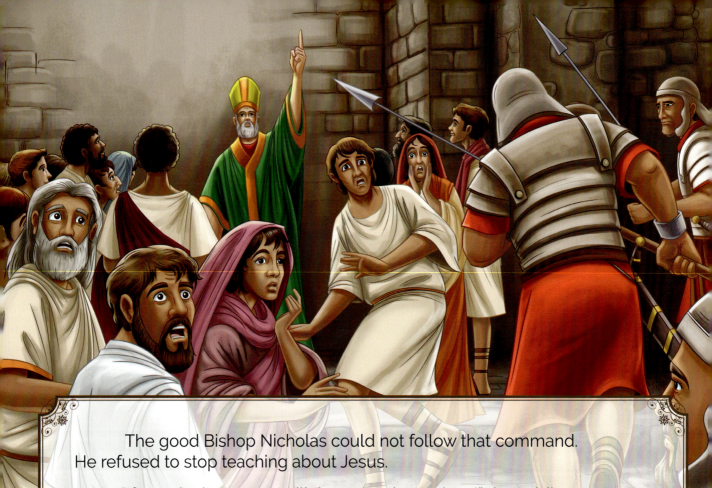

The good Bishop Nicholas could not follow that command. He refused to stop teaching about Jesus.

"If you don't stop, we will throw you into prison!" the soldiers threatened him.

But Nicholas would look at them and say, "How could I turn my back on God? Should I stop talking about His goodness just because you might throw me into prison? Jesus gave His life for me. Should I not be willing to do the same for Him?"

The soldiers were surprised to hear Nicholas say that, but because he would not stop his teaching, they threw him in prison.

For years, Nicholas remained in prison, but he continued to be true to God. Finally, a new Roman leader came into power and set all the Christian prisoners free. Bishop Nicholas was at liberty to serve his people again, and he did so with all his heart. He was now older and a bit more tired, but that would not stop him from doing his best.

That is why it was a surprise to him when he met a church leader named Arius who was teaching bad things. Arius was telling people that Jesus was not the Son of God.

Nicholas wasted no time correcting the church leader, but Arius would not back down. Nicholas loved Jesus very much. He had even gone to prison for his faith. When Arius would not stop teaching bad things about Jesus, Nicholas lost his temper and slapped him!

Because of that, Nicholas was punished. He could no longer be a bishop. Walking away by himself, he sat down near a pine tree, and what do you think he did?

"Lord, I'm sorry," he prayed. "I should not have lost my temper. What am I going to do now? I wanted to give You everything… now I have nothing to give."

Then a thought came to him.

"What am I saying? Why, I have a lot to give You! I don't have a job but I have all the time in the world to serve You!"

Soon, Nicholas could be seen going everywhere, sharing everything he had with those in need and helping them in any way he could. He gave out food and clothing and even toys. He carried them in a sack, and just like he did when he was a child, he made sure no one was watching when he left gifts for people.

Good Nicholas was soon known as Saint Nicholas, or Saint Nick for short. He did everything he could to help the poor and needy and even built homes for poor orphans.

He didn't have money, but he gave what he had—himself.

"Keep in mind the words of the Lord Jesus who said, *It is more blessed to give than to receive.*"

Acts 20:35

Enjoy your holidays with stories about the people we celebrate:

The Holiday Saints book collection!

Stories of the people whose dedication to God
helped to change the world.

For more books like this one, visit:
www.brotherfrancisonline.com